REMAINS TO BE SEEN

EXPLORING ANCIENT EGYPT

JOHN MALAM

EVANS BROTHERS LIMITED

This book is based on **Indiana Jones Explores Ancient Egypt,**
first published in 1991.

Evans Brothers Limited
2A Portman Mansions
Chiltern Street
London W1M 1LE

© text and illustrations Evans Brothers Limited in this edition 1997

Reprinted 1999, 1999

Printed in Spain by GRAFO, S.A. -Bilbao

ISBN 0 237 51839 2

Acknowledgements

The author and publishers would like to thank the following people
for their valuable help and advice:

Dr John Taylor, a curator in the Department of Egyptian Antiqui-
ties, the British Museum
Margaret Sharman, author and archaeologist
Peter A. Clayton, lecturer in Egyptology and writer

Illustrations: Jeffery Burn
Maps and diagrams: Jillie Luff, Bitmap Graphics

Editor: Jean Coppendale
Design: Neil Sayer
Production: Jenny Mulvanny

For permission to reproduce copyright material the author and
publishers gratefully acknowledge the following:

Cover photograph: James Morris

Title page: reproduced by Courtesy of the Trustees of the British
Museum

page 6 Robert Harding Picture Library **page 8** Peter A. Clayton
page 9 Bernard Regent, The Hutchison Library **page 10** (top) Peter
A. Clayton, (bottom) reproduced by courtesy of the Trustees of the
British Museum **page 11** (top) Werner Forman Archive/The
Ashmolean Museum, Oxford, (bottom) Peter A. Clayton **pages 12-
14** Peter A. Clayton **page 15** Robert Harding Picture Library **page
16** (top) Peter A. Clayton, (bottom) reproduced by courtesy of the
Trustees of the British Museum **page 17** (top) Peter A. Clayton,
(bottom) James Morris **page 18** F. Jackson, Robert Harding Picture
Library **pages 19-22** Peter A. Clayton **page 23** Robert Harding
Picture Library **page 24** reproduced by courtesy of the Trustees of
the British Museum **page 26** (bottom left) reproduced by courtesy
of the Trustees of the British Museum, (bottom right) Peter A.
Clayton **page 27** (top left) James Morris, (top right) Peter A.
Clayton, (bottom left) Robert Harding Picture Library (bottom right)
Peter A. Clayton **page 28** reproduced by courtesy of the Trustees of
the British Museum **page 30** Peter A. Clayton **page 31** (top) Terry
Spencer, Colorific! (bottom left) Peter A. Clayton, (bottom right)
Terry Spencer, Colorific! **page 32** (left) E.T. Archive, (right) Peter A.
Clayton **page 33** (top left) Werner Forman Archive/Berlin, (top
right) Werner Forman Archive/Egyptian Museum, Cairo, (bottom)
Peter A. Clayton **pages 34-35** Robert Harding Picture Library **page
36** Robert Harding Picture Library **page 37** (top left) Robert
Harding Picture Library, (top right) Illustrated London News,
(middle) Peter A. Clayton, (bottom) Illustrated London News **page
38** Robert Harding Picture Library **page 39** (top) E. T. Archive
(bottom) Robert Harding Picture Library **page 40** (left) Robert
Harding Picture Library, (right) James Morris **page 41** Robert
Harding Picture Library **page 42** (top) Peter A. Clayton, (bottom
left) reproduced by courtesy of the Trustees of the British Museum,
(bottom right) John G. Ross, Robert Harding Picture Library **page
43** Robert Harding Picture Library **page 44** Peter A. Clayton **page
45** (top left) John G. Ross, Robert Harding Picture Library, (right)
Robert Harding Picture Library

Contents

TIMELINE OF ANCIENT EGYPT
and the rest of the world

5000 BC

4000 BC

Earliest writing developed in
Mesopotamia
(Modern Iran and Iraq)

3000 BC

Stonehenge begun in England

Indus Valley civilization begins
(Modern Pakistan and India)

2000 BC

Minoan civilization on Crete begins
(first European civilization)

1000 BC

Parthenon built in Athens

Great Wall of China finished

Birth of Jesus Christ

0 BC

Colosseum built in Rome

AD 0

End of Roman Empire in the west

Civilizations in Central and
South America (Aztec, Maya,
Toltec)

AD 1000

Christopher Columbus
discovers America

Captain Cook
discovers Australia

AD 2000

		5000 BC
PREDYNASTIC PERIOD	A lengthy, prehistoric time. A time before Egypt was ruled by pharaohs. Small communities of farmers settled along the River Nile and built villages.	
		3100 BC
ARCHAIC PERIOD	Narmer brought the two parts of Egypt together. He was probably Egypt's first pharaoh and began the first dynasty.	Dynasties 1 and 2
		2650 BC
OLD KINGDOM	The age of pyramid building. Pyramids and Sphinx at Giza built.	Dynasties 3 to 10
		2050 BC
MIDDLE KINGDOM	The last of the pyramids built.	Dynasties 11 to 17
		1550 BC
NEW KINGDOM	Pharaohs buried in the Valley of the Kings. Akhenaten built a new city in the desert. Tutankhamun returned to the old capital. Ramesses II at war with the Hittites.	Dynasties 18 to 25
		700 BC
LATE PERIOD	The last Egyptian pharaohs ruled Egypt.	Dynasties 26 to 31
		332 BC
GREEK AND ROMAN PERIOD	Alexander the Great brought Egypt into the Greek empire and built his city at Alexandria. In 30 BC Egypt became part of the Roman empire.	AD 395

Dates

Egyptian history is usually given the dates of the various dynasties and pharaohs. Another way of writing dates is to refer to things before and after the birth of Jesus Christ. Anything before is said to be 'BC' (Before Christ), and anything after is 'AD' (**Anno Domini**, which is Latin for 'in the year of our Lord').

WHO WERE THE EGYPTIANS?

Introduction to Ancient Egypt

In the north of Africa is a hot, dry country which today we call Egypt. To the Ancient Greeks it was **Aigyptos**, and to the Romans it was **Aegyptus.** It is the land of the pharaohs. Egypt is a vast sandy desert through which flows the River Nile. It was along the narrow, fertile strip made by that great river that the civilization of Ancient Egypt flourished for more than 3,000 years. On this same ribbon of land today lives 96 per cent of the modern population of Egypt.

Ancient Egypt was one of the first great civilizations of the world and it influenced many cultures which developed later in the Mediterranean area. The Egyptians influenced both the Greeks and the Romans.

'Civilization' is an important word which is used by historians to describe the world of the Ancient Egyptians. Put simply, it means that people's lives had reached an advanced stage of development. We can see this today in what remains of Ancient Egyptian art and architecture. From their own writing, and that of ancient visitors to Egypt, we can learn about Egyptian religion and the lives of the people. When all this information is gathered together it reveals a single, united culture. It was the people of this culture who were the real Ancient Egyptians.

Fact File

The River Nile

This is quite a river! It's 6,671 kilometres long and it's the longest river in Africa. The Ancient Egyptians depended on the River Nile for their living. It flooded once a year in August and September, and in the flood-water was a rich black mud washed down from the mountains of Ethiopia. After the flood, the mud was left along the river banks. It was here that the Egyptians farmed and built their towns. The fertile mud was so important that the Egyptians named their country after it. They called it 'Kemet', which meant 'the Black Land'.

The fertile strip by the banks of the River Nile with the pyramids of Giza in the background. The civilization of Ancient Egypt developed along this narrow piece of land.

Mediterranean
Sea

Rosetta

Alexandria

Delta
of the
Nile

Bubastis

LOWER
EGYPT

Cairo

Giza

Memphis

River Nile

N

Akhetaten
(Tell el-Amarna)

Find your way in
Ancient Egypt

Red Sea

Abydos

Nagada

Valley of the Kings

Karnak

Deir el-Medina

Thebes

0   km   200

UPPER
EGYPT

Ancient Egypt

Aswan

Fertile strip

Abu Simbel

ANCIENT
EGYPT

MODERN
EGYPT

R. Nile

Ancient Egypt

Boundary of
Egypt today

Egypt before the pharaohs

This pot was made by the Amratian people, ancestors of the Ancient Egyptians. The decoration shows a drawing of a Nile boat.

When we think of Ancient Egypt today, it is very tempting only to remember the achievements of the civilization. We might only think about 'mummies', 'pharaohs' or 'pyramids'. But what was it like in the time before these became important to the Egyptians?

The earliest inhabitants of Egypt lived along the River Nile about 12,000 years ago. They caught fish in the river and gathered wild cereals. Because they were hunters and gatherers they did not have permanent settlements, only temporary camp-sites.

Around 7,000 years ago changes took place when some of these people settled down and began to farm the land. They planted wild wheat seeds and cultivated the cereal plants which grew. By choosing seeds from healthy plants their crops became strong and gave a good return of grain. Wild sheep and cattle were tamed and gradually they became domesticated animals. These early Egyptians learned how to live in villages. Among the people were farmers, potters, weavers, carpenters and stone-workers.

The time before the pharaohs was a prehistoric time – a time when there was no writing. The origins of the Ancient Egyptians can be traced back to this remote period and about 5,000 years ago the first signs of Egyptian civilization began to appear.

Fact File

A prehistoric burial

This is one of the ancestors of the Ancient Egyptians. People were given simple burials, usually in pits dug into the ground (see page 26). They were often buried with pots containing food for the afterlife. This person died over 5,000 years ago and was buried in a crouching position inside a coffin made from reeds from the River Nile.

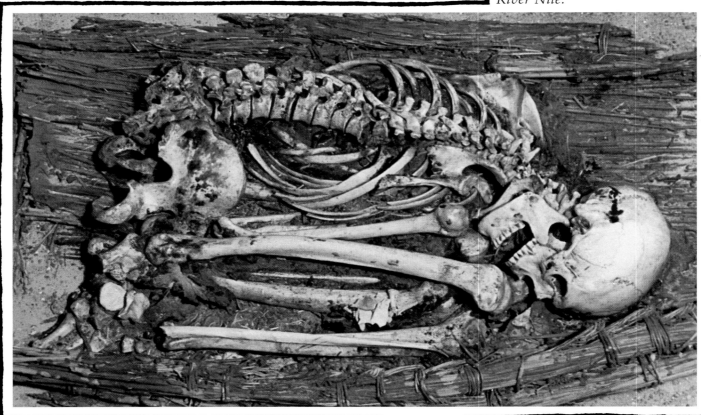

Objects from before the time of the pharaohs

The 'Two Dogs Palette' made of green slate with a carving of two leaping hunting dogs on either side.

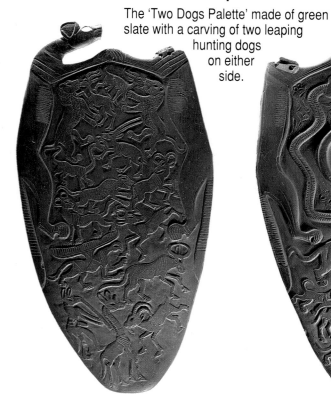

A flat cosmetic palette made of slate. These palettes ranged from simple rectangular shapes to elegant forms often in the shapes of birds, fish or animals. They were used to grind or mix eye paints.

36368

An unusual terracotta (pottery) figure holding a large ingot (brick) probably of copper.

An ivory hair comb. Elaborate handles were fashionable and were often carved into the figures of animals or birds.

A selection of three flints. The two knife-shaped flints would probably have been used for skinning animals or cutting food. The bottom flint is an arrow-head.

The dynasties of Ancient Egypt

The prehistoric villages of Egypt grew into small towns. About 5,000 years ago two large kingdoms emerged, one in the north of the country (called Lower Egypt) and the other in the south (called Upper Egypt). Each kingdom had its own capital and was ruled by a king.

A story about early Egypt tells of a ruler called Menes. According to legend, he was extremely powerful and under him the two kingdoms were brought together and united. Egyptian rulers were given more than one name and some people think that Menes was another name for Narmer, Egypt's first king, who we know about from ancient inscriptions.

Narmer has a very important place in the history of Ancient Egypt. Not only did he unite the two kingdoms but he also founded the first Egyptian royal family. For nearly 3,000 years after Narmer, Egypt was ruled by kings (and very occasionally a queen). The kings can be placed in family groups which are called 'dynasties'. In all, there were 31 dynasties with about 125 important kings and many less important ones. Another name for an Ancient Egyptian king is 'pharaoh' which comes from the word 'per-ao'. This was the Egyptian word for the royal palace of the king.

This is part of the 'king list' from the temple of Ramesses II at Abydos. It names many pharaohs and is a guide to the rulers of Ancient Egypt.

Crowns of Egypt. The White Crown was worn by the ruler of Upper Egypt and the Red Crown by the ruler of Lower Egypt. After Narmer united the two kingdoms one crown was worn, made up of both the old crowns. The Double Crown showed that one king ruled over both kingdoms. Blue was considered to be a 'royal colour' and later rulers used the Blue Crown and the Double Crown. The Atef Crown was the most elaborate crown which was worn by the king on special occasions. It is also often pictured being worn by the god Osiris. It has the White Crown in the centre with ostrich feathers on either side and ram's horns at the base. Egyptian queens had their own headdresses which were worn on special occasions.

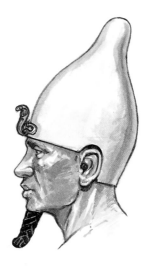
White Crown

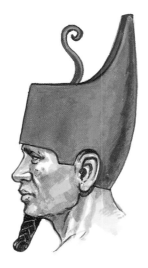
Red Crown

Fact File

Narmer's Palette

Here is one of the most important objects from Ancient Egypt. Historians still argue about its meaning, 100 years after it was found. This slate, usually called a 'palette' (because it looks like a stone for mixing make-up on), is carved on both sides. It tells the story of a battle, in pictures. On one side a victorious king strikes his fallen enemy with a stone mace and on the other side he inspects two rows of headless bodies. The name of Narmer appears, the first king to rule the whole of Egypt. This palette might have been made to celebrate Narmer uniting the two parts of Egypt into one land.

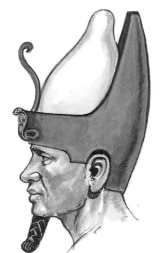

Double Crown

Blue Crown

Atef Crown

THE WORLD OF THE PHARAOHS

Egypt under the pharaohs

For 3,000 years Egypt was ruled by pharaohs. Historians have divided this long time into three main periods. The first group of pharaohs belonged to what is called the 'Old Kingdom'. They were followed by the pharaohs of the 'Middle Kingdom' and the last group reigned in the 'New Kingdom'.

An Egyptian pharaoh was more than just a king. To the Ancient Egyptians he was a god who had come to live among them. It is very difficult for us to understand this today because the kings and queens of the modern world are not thought of like this at all.

Only the pharaoh had the power to talk to the gods and it was he who ordered that temples and other buildings were built for them. The temples were decorated according to the pharaoh's personal instructions. He was held responsible for the wealth and success of the country and in times of trouble only he could put things right. After his death the pharaoh was said to have actually joined the gods for the sole purpose of helping his people.

As king of Egypt the pharaoh was leader of the army, head of religion and in charge of government. There were officials to help him carry out his duties. According to a story about Ramesses III, over 62,000 people worked for him in just one of his temples and on the large amount of land that belonged to it! They were farmers, builders, priests and musicians. Ramesses III paid a high price for being pharaoh – he was murdered by some of his own officials.

Detail of a wall painting in the tomb of a young prince. It shows the prince's father, Ramesses III, wearing the tall White Crown.

A view of the main gateway of the mortuary temple of Ramesses III. Such temples were built for the cult, or worship, of the dead king.

Fact File

The Sphinx

What strange creature is this? Half lion, half human, it seems to stand guard over the group of pyramids at Giza. It is carved from a small hill of limestone and the head is thought to represent one of Ancient Egypt's early pharaohs, Khafre. Once it was painted red and yellow and traces of paint can still be found on the head. Until recently the Sphinx was buried by sand but now this has been taken away the figure is starting to fall apart. No one really knows what the word 'sphinx' means. It might come from Egyptian words meaning 'living image'.

Life in Ancient Egypt

Egyptian society was very organized and everyone had a part to play in it. Men and women were treated equally. There were many different jobs to do and no matter what the work was, it was done for the pharaoh. There were farmers, weavers, painters, writers, potters, jewellers and priests. The products of their work were for the enjoyment of the pharaoh and through their skills Egyptian civilization reached great heights.

The system of government was very complicated, and it needed many officials to carry out the day-to-day duties of the state. These duties were performed by the ordinary people. The most important official was the vizier. He was called the 'chief of all the pharaoh's works'. The vizier gave orders to other officials. He made sure all parts of the government were working well.

Ordinary Egyptians believed that their position in life was given to them by the gods and it could not be changed. So, a person born a slave remained a slave all their life. But later, the rules that governed everyday life changed and it became possible for people to better themselves. Even so, no matter what a person's position was, they were still there for the good of the pharaoh and the gods.

A wooden model of two papyrus boats (skiffs) trawling a net between them to catch fish in the River Nile. Fishermen also used spears to catch larger fish.

Jewellers at work, 1400BC, from an Egyptian tomb painting.

Fact File

What did they wear?

We know a lot about the clothes of the Ancient Egyptians from the pictures they painted of themselves. White linen, made by village weavers from fibres of the flax plant, was the most common material. Tailors made it into short 'kilts' and loin cloths for the men and long dresses for the women. Leather or woven reed sandals were worn on the feet. Coloured fabrics were hardly ever worn because the dyes used would come out in the wash. Children wore few clothes and in paintings are often shown naked and with their heads shaved except for locks of hair called 'locks of youth'.

Everyday clothing of the Egyptians. The two children have shaved heads with 'locks of youth'.

This wall painting shows an Egyptian family on a papyrus boat in the marshes at the edge of the River Nile. The man is called Nebamun, and with his wife, daughter and cat he is hunting for birds. He holds three herons in one hand and a snake-shaped throwing stick in the other.

An Egyptian village

In the past, historians who studied the civilization of Ancient Egypt were only interested in the remains of buildings that had been built for the pharaohs and other important people. They hoped to find precious objects from long ago. Today, archaeologists search for the places where ordinary people lived. The idea is to learn as much as possible about them. After all, it was through the work of ordinary Egyptians that Ancient Egypt became a great civilization.

One village that has been studied is at Deir el-Medina, a cluster of stone and mud-brick houses. In the village lived the crafts-people responsible for making and decorating the royal tombs in the Valley of the Kings. The village had one main street and was surrounded by a strong wall which was patrolled by guards whose job it was to keep watch on the community. The houses were long and thin with four small rooms built in a row, one after the other. They had cellars and flat roofs. Deir el-Medina was inhabited for 500 years.

Not all villages were like Deir el-Medina. Villages near the River Nile would have been made of sun-dried mud-brick or pole-and-mud houses and the people who lived in them would have been free to come and go as they wished.

Inside a painted tomb at Deir el-Medina. This tomb belonged to the chief artist to Ramesses II.

The tomb-workers' village of Deir el-Medina was built in a waterless valley. It was buried by sand until the early 1800s when fragments of ancient objects were discovered. It was uncovered between 1922 and 1951 and has provided a remarkable source of information about the lives of ordinary Egyptians.

Fact File

Village life

Deir el-Medina must have been very smelly! For a start, the houses were packed closely together and the one street in the village seems to have been covered over which would have made the place hot, dark and airless.

If that wasn't bad enough, the floors of the houses were filthy. When the village was excavated the house floors were found to be piled deep with goat, sheep and pig droppings!

To amuse themselves, the skilled painters in the village would draw little pictures of everyday life, often on fragments of limestone. This one here shows two girls cleaning out a big pot. It's an Ancient Egyptian doodle!

Boats on the Nile

The River Nile was very important to the Ancient Egyptians. Not only did its flood-waters bring soil for farming (see page 8), but people depended on the river for transport. Travel by boat was part of evryday life.

The first boats to sail on the Nile were simple rafts made from bundles of papyrus stalks held together with rope. It was a boat like this which the hunter Nebamun used when he went in search of birds (see page 17). It was easy to make and could be easily replaced.

Stronger boats were made of wood specially brought by traders from the Lebanon. Special boats, such as the barges used on state occasions, were sometimes made of cedar. All boats were flat-bottomed, and passengers, crew and cargo were carried on deck.

Sailing up the Nile (heading south) was easier than sailing downstream (north). This was because boats were usually helped by a good wind if they went upstream and they had sails to catch the wind. But travelling north meant sailing into the wind and for these journeys paddles or oars had to be used.

The boats of the Egyptian navy were used more for moving troops and goods than for actual warfare. The naval fleet was based at Memphis and from here it was sent out on trading expeditions to foreign lands. After one trip, the boats of Hatshepsut, a queen of the 18th Dynasty, returned from the land of Punt laden with ivory, ebony, incense, eye-cosmetics, monkeys, dogs and panther skins. Punt was possibly modern-day Somalia, reached by sailing down the Red Sea and into the Indian Ocean.

Fact File

Boat of the Sun

Imagine uncovering a 4,500-year-old boat buried in the desert! In 1954 that's just what happened when the Egyptologist Kamal el-Mallakh explored an area at the foot of the pyramid of Khufu. He found a gigantic pit inside which was a dismantled boat. There were 1,224 pieces of cedar and it took many years to put the boat back together. It was huge, measuring 44 metres long and 6 metres wide. But what was it used for? It was probably a ceremonial boat used by the pharaoh Khufu. It may also have been the boat which, according to tradition, carried the Sun through the heavens.

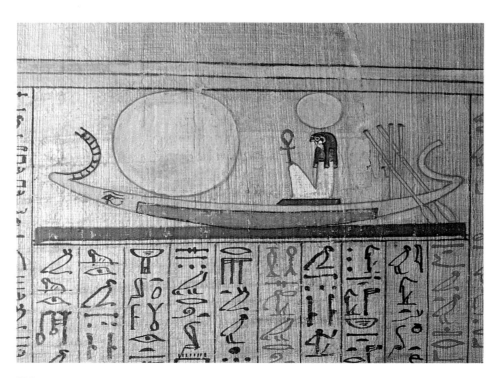

The Sun crossing the sky in a boat with the sitting figure of the sun god Re. This drawing is from 'The Book of the Dead'– see page 24.

This large boat would have been a familiar sight on the Nile 3,300 years ago, in the time of queen Hatshepsut. A boat such as this would have been used for sea-going journeys to countries which Egypt traded with. It had two large rudder oars, operated by a helmsman, and a sail more wide than tall. Goods were held in the central deckhouse as well as being carried on the open deck.

Ancient Egypt at war

The Egyptian army was led by the pharaoh or one of his sons. It was very well organised. Soldiers were grouped into divisions of 5,000 fighting men. There were smaller groups within the divisions, each with 50 men.

The army was made up of soldiers who had joined as volunteers, and others who had been ordered to join. Some soldiers were slaves. They could gain their freedom by fighting on the side of the Egyptians.

Soldiers fought with swords, axes and spears. Archers fired arrows with stone or metal points.

A soldier carrying a shield made of ox-hide and an axe with a curved blade.

Three foreign soldiers of Ramesses II's army. They are wearing horned helmets and carrying short swords and shields.

It is difficult to find out all the details about Ancient Egypt at war because the Egyptians only recorded their victories, not their defeats. And when the victories were written down, sometimes years after the events, the truth was likely to be changed. Over the years a defeat could become a victory and a minor victory could become a boastful account of a great battle. Changing facts like this was intended to gain support for the pharaoh and make him into a great leader.

Perhaps the first record of a battle is the one represented on Narmer's Palette (see page 13). The headless bodies pictured on one side of the palette were probably the bodies of a defeated enemy.

The battles of Ramesses II against the Hittites are well recorded. The Hittites were from Anatolia, in what is now Turkey. At the battle of Kadesh, a Hittite town in Syria, Ramesses II is said to have won a famous victory in the year 1285BC. A peace treaty was signed and the daughter of the Hittite king was sent to join Ramesses II as his wife. Just to show how confusing military history can be, a copy of the same treaty, found in the Hittite capital Boghazköy, said the battle of Kadesh was their victory! Ramesses II was thought to be a great pharaoh by the Ancient Egyptians, as his giant statues at the temple of Abu Simbel reveal (see page 31).

Fact File

The war chariot

Tuthmosis IV had a chariot decorated with pictures of himself as a mighty warrior, fighting his enemies in battle. Tutankhamun had a box painted with similar scenes which showed him firing long arrows from his chariot. But in both cases there is no real evidence that these battles ever took place! They may just be pictures of how the pharaohs wanted to be seen – as strong and powerful leaders. The two-wheeled war chariots were made from wood, with some leather and metal. They held two men, the driver (or charioteer) and the chariot warrior and were pulled by a pair of horses.

Tutankhamun in his war chariot. This painting was found on the side of a wooden box in the pharaoh's tomb. It shows the boy king fighting an Asian enemy. To the right a soldier is cutting the hand off a dead enemy. This was how the number of people killed in battle were counted. Inside the box were several pairs of the pharaoh's sandals.

GODS AND RELIGION

Death and burial in Ancient Egypt

Try and imagine what it must have been like inside an embalmer's workshop. It was hot and smelly and would have been buzzing with flies! The workshop, which was actually a special sort of tent, was where the body of a dead person was prepared for what the Ancient Egyptians called the 'afterlife'. They believed that the spirit of a dead person travelled to a kind of heavenly Egypt where it would live forever. But before this could happen, many important ceremonies had to be performed. The most important was to preserve the body and make sure it didn't decay. This is where the embalmers came in!

Mummification is the word used to describe the process of preserving a body by embalming it. Take a look over there on the right. Laid out on the table is the corpse. Soon after death, the liver, stomach, lungs and intestines were removed and placed in special containers called canopic jars. The brain was extracted through the nostrils. The heart was left in the body. Then the empty body cavity and skull were packed with preservatives. Finally, the body was bathed in oils and perfumes before being covered with natron (a kind of soda), salt and molten resin which dried the corpse. Sometimes, false eyes were inserted and the lips and cheeks painted with rouge. All this was to make the corpse look as life-like as possible!

A mummy wrapped in layers of bandages inside its painted coffin. Over 1,000 mummies are known to exist and archaeologists examine them to find out about the diseases they might have suffered from when they were alive, what sort of food they ate and how old they were when they died. It's amazing what you can learn from an ancient body!

The complete process of mummification, including wrapping up the body with long linen bandages, took 70 days. Good luck charms were often placed between the layers of bandage and each finger and toe was wrapped separately. A mask showing a likeness of the dead person was then placed on the head of the mummy. The masks of pharaohs were made from pure gold (see page 35). The mummy was then put inside one or more painted coffins and buried in a specially made tomb.

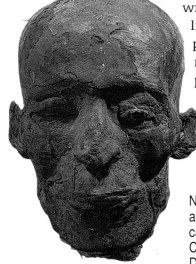

Head of a mummy.

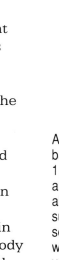

Not only people were mummified! This is a mummy of a cat. At the town of Bubastis cats were regarded as sacred animals. Cat cemeteries have been found there. Dogs and other animals were also embalmed and wrapped in bandages.

The Book of the Dead

The journey to the afterlife was full of troubles for the spirit of a dead person. To make it easier, a collection of about 200 magic spells was written called the 'Book of the Dead'. Some spells were written on papyrus which could be wrapped between the bandages of a mummy, near its legs. Spell 31, for example, was to protect the spirit from demons which came in the form of reptiles. Part of it said, 'Get away from me! Stay away, you evil one!...O you who would speak against this magic of mine, no crocodile who lives on magic will take it away from me!'

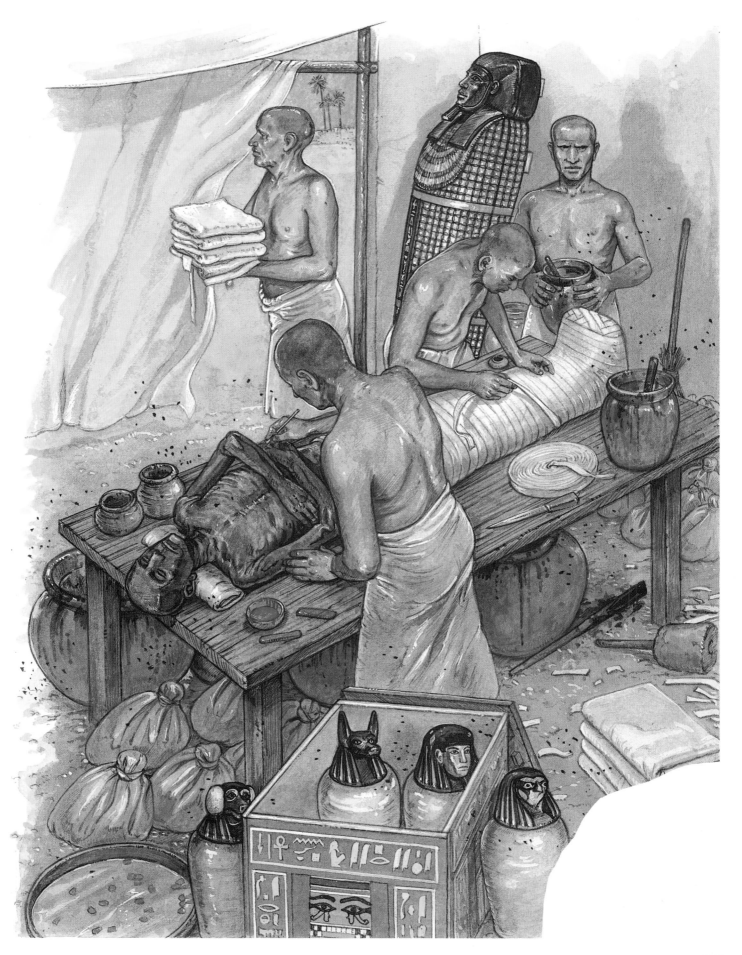

The age of pyramids

For 1,000 years pharaohs were buried in special tombs which we call pyramids. About 90 pyramids are known today and the best preserved are the ones at Giza, near Cairo, the modern capital of Egypt.

The pyramids at Giza were built 4,500 years ago during the reigns of the pharaohs Khufu, Khafre and Menkaure (some people use the Greek versions of their names – Cheops, Chephren and Mycerinus). The pyramid built for Khufu was the largest ever made. More than two million huge blocks of limestone were used in his pyramid. When it was finished, after 20 years' work, it stood 146 metres high – the tallest building ever at that time. The Giza pyramids were the first of the 'Seven Wonders of the World'.

To build the pyramids at Giza, massive blocks of limestone, each weighing about two tonnes, came on barges which sailed along the River Nile. Canals brought the barges to the building site at Giza. Then, gangs of men used ropes and wooden rollers to drag the blocks up slopes of mud-brick, until they could fix each block into the right place in the pyramid.

This is the group of pyramids at Giza. At the top of the pyramid of Khafre are traces of its smooth limestone facing.

How pyramids developed

1) **6,000 years ago.** Egyptians were buried in pits.

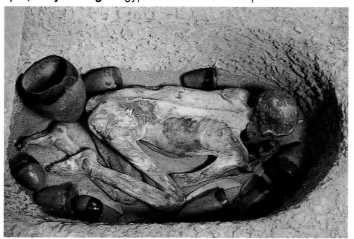

2) **5,000 years ago.** Kings and nobles were buried in pits which were covered over by a mud-brick platform. These are called 'mastaba' tombs.

Check its size

CN Tower,
Toronto
(555m)

Pyramid of Khufu,
Giza (146m)

Statue of Liberty,
New York (93m)

Fact File

Valley of the Kings

You know what the problem with pyramids was? They were easy to rob. Tomb robbers broke into the pyramids and stole all they could carry. They even unwrapped the mummies to look for gold charms. So, the later pharaohs were buried in tombs cut into rock. One of the most sacred places to be buried was the Valley of the Kings. The tombs here were made by the workers from the nearby village of Deir el-Medina. The tombs were decorated with paintings and filled with objects and treasures to help the dead person in the afterlife. But, tomb robbers broke in and stole all they held – except for Tutankhamun's tomb (see page 34).

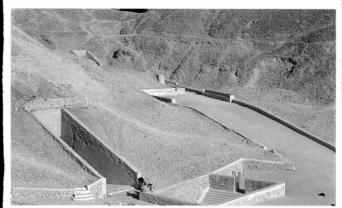

Entrances to the tombs of Ramesses VI and Tutankhamun, in the Valley of the Kings.

3) 4,600 years ago. The first pyramid was built by the architect Imhotep, for the pharaoh Djoser. This was the so-called Step Pyramid. It began as a mastaba tomb to which Imhotep added several raised platforms in stone.

4) 4,500 years ago. The true pyramid had arrived. This is the pyramid of Khafre.

Gods of the Ancient Egyptians

Throughout the entire history of Ancient Egypt there was no single system of religion. Instead there were many different ideas and lots of gods and goddesses to worship. At different times in Egyptian history certain gods were more popular than others. Each town worshipped its own favourite gods, who might be completely unknown in the town next door. Temples were built for the gods to live in (see page 30).

Anubis was one of the most ancient of the gods. He had the head of a jackal and his purpose was to oversee the mummification and bandaging of a body and then guide it to the afterlife.

Fact File

Working for the gods

In case the gods ordered the dead person to work for them, he was buried with hundreds of tiny figures. These are called 'ushabtis' after the Egyptian word 'usheb' which means 'answer'. So, if the gods told the dead person to work, then his ushabtis could answer for him and carry it out.

In wealthy tombs there were 401 ushabtis – one for each day of the year (365) and 36 overseers to organize the worker ushabtis! But in poorer tombs there were fewer. Most were made from stone, wood or a glazed material called faience and inscribed on the front with a spell (to make the ushabti work) or just the name of the dead person.

A ushabti figure about 40 centimetres high. She is holding a hoe and a sickle for use in the afterlife. On her front is a spell from the 'Book of the Dead'.

Horus was worshipped in most places as a sun god. He had the head of a falcon and in paintings he is shown wearing the Double Crown of Egypt.

Osiris was shown wrapped as a mummy wearing the White Crown. In the afterlife he was the judge of the dead. The dead person's heart was weighed against a likeness of the goddess Maat, who represented truth and justice. If the heart and the image of the goddess balanced, the owner could enter the afterlife. But if they did not balance then the owner could not enter.

Isis was the sister of Osiris, whom she married. Their child became the god Horus. Isis was worshipped as the protector of children. She was usually shown wearing cow's horns between which rested the sacred disc of the sun.

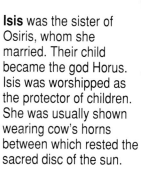

Thoth was the god of learning and science. He was said to be the inventor of writing (look for the writing implement in his hand). He was shown with the head of an ibis, which was a bird found along the River Nile.

Bastet was a cat-headed goddess worshipped in the town of Bubastis, where cats were regarded as sacred.

Temples of Ancient Egypt

Many temples have survived in good condition. This shows how much importance was attached to them, whereas the homes of ordinary people disappeared thousands of years ago, leaving barely a trace behind.

Temples were built for the gods. The Egyptians thought of them as 'houses' for the gods to live in, and it was here where the pharaoh could talk to them. Since the pharaoh was thought of as a god himself, he was regarded as equal to them. Every town had its own temple dedicated to the town's gods.

In all parts of Egypt, temples were built to the same basic shape, just like churches are today. The temple of Amun-Re, at Karnak, was one of the greatest temples ever built. This temple was massive, covering two hectares. Each new pharaoh added buildings which is why the complex became so grand. It had six gateways, one after the other, some of which rose 30 metres into the sky. Covered halls contained hundreds of tightly packed columns painted with bold designs. An excavation in 1903 found 17,000 small statues buried at the bottom of a deep pit. It seems the temple had been cleaned up and a pharaoh had ordered old statues to be removed.

The temple of Amun-Re (left), at Karnak, where the largest hall of columns (above) was bigger than the biggest cathedral in Europe.

Take a look at the photographs on this page. These are the ruins of Amun-Re's temple, but try and imagine it filled with priests worshipping their god, saying their prayers and singing hymns in his praise.

Fact File

Abu Simbel temple

Can you believe what happened to this beautiful temple? When the Egyptian government decided to build a dam at Aswan, it looked as if this 3,000-year-old mountain of red sandstone was going to be lost beneath a new lake. An international appeal was started and in 1960 workmen began to reconstruct the Abu Simbel temple on high ground, above the flood-water of the new Lake Nasser. Inside an artificial hill they made a concrete dome to house the old temple and at the front they rebuilt the four enormous figures of the seated pharaoh, Ramesses II. Each figure had to be cut into blocks before it could be moved to its new location above the lake.

Rebuilding the temple of Abu Simbel.

TWO DIFFERENT PHARAOHS

Egypt in the reign of Akhenaten

It's hard to decide if Akhenaten was a wise or a foolish pharaoh. He was pharaoh for 17 years during the 18th Dynasty, 3,350 years ago, and in this time he brought many changes to the lives of his people. He was a thinker. He thought and did things differently from other pharaohs. He changed the religion and moved the capital to a new city.

In the early years of his reign, Akhenaten was called Amenophis IV. He became known as Akhenaten when he abandoned the old religion, which had many gods, and replaced it with the worship of just one god. This god was called Aten, the sun god, and Akhenaten took the god's name for his own name. He ordered the names of the old gods to be removed from the temples – an act which would have confused and upset many people.

There were also artistic changes during the reign of Akhenaten. The artists of the day showed their pharaoh with very distinctive features – large fleshy thighs, a chubby stomach and a long, thin head.

Fact File

City in the sand

Akhenaten really did have different ideas. Who else would have built a new capital in the desert, 300 kilometres down the Nile from the old city of Thebes? His new capital, called Akhetaten, was dedicated to the sun god, Aten. Within a few years it was ready and Akhenaten and his family moved in. The temples at Thebes were closed and some people moved north to new homes. But Akhenaten's city did not last very long, perhaps no more than 15 years. After he died people moved back to their old homes and the new city was covered by the desert. Today, the site is named after two local villages and is called Tell el-Amarna.

The ruins of the North Palace at Akhetaten, Akhenaten's capital.

Akhenaten, Nefertiti and their children worshipping the sun god.

Akhenaten may have looked like this in real life – see for yourself from the pictures here. If he did look like this, it was strange that his artists chose not to portray him in a more flattering way. But perhaps he did not look like this at all and what we see in the statues and paintings today is the result of a surprising new art style.

Nefertiti, wife of Akhenaten, and possibly ruler of Egypt for a short time after his death. She had six children, all girls.

The unusual features of Akhenaten. His mummy has not been found, otherwise it would be possible to reconstruct his appearance from the remains of his body. Some people say it was destroyed not long after he was buried. No one really knows.

Egypt in the reign of Tutankhamun

This pharaoh is just about the most famous person from the time of Ancient Egypt. But remember, Tutankhamun is one of the most mysterious pharaohs and archaeologists still need to find out more about him before they can be sure they know him really well. His is the richest tomb to have been found in modern times and despite this little is known about him.

He was a son-in-law of Akhenaten. He came to the throne after Akhenaten and was only nine years old when he became pharaoh. At first he was called Tutankhaten, carrying on the tradition of Akhenaten that pharaohs should have the name of Aten, the sun god, as part of their own name. He also worshipped one god only and his capital was at Tell el-Amarna. But all this was to change.

Within three years of becoming pharaoh, the young king changed his name to Tutankhamun. By doing this he went back to the old style of religion practised before Akhenaten. The old gods were worshipped once more and the temples in the religious capital of Thebes which had been closed for 20 years were re-opened. He left Tell el-Amarna to be covered by the desert sand and moved to the old administrative capital of Memphis, near Cairo. After the experiments of Akhenaten, Tutankhamun went back to the 'old ways of life' and apart from this not much more is known about him.

He died aged 18 or 19 years old and his early death (possibly from an injury to the head) brought the 18th Dynasty almost to a close, 3,300 years ago. He was buried in a small tomb and his coffin was surrounded by thousands of objects intended for his use in the afterlife.

Tutankhamun's magnificent golden throne.

Fact File

Burying the pharaoh
Tutankhamun might not have been a great pharaoh, but his priests made sure he had a spectacular funeral. In between the bandages were placed 143 precious gold and jewelled objects. A mask of solid gold was placed over his face. The mummy was then put into three coffins, the innermost made of solid gold, and placed in a tomb in the Valley of the Kings. The tomb was filled with all the things he might need for the afterlife such as his clothes and personal jewellery, his furniture (including his bed), chariots and games. Then the great doors were closed and sealed.

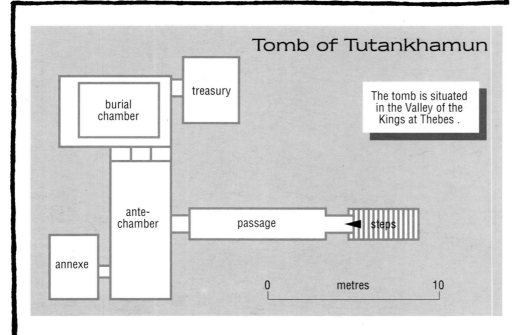

Tomb of Tutankhamun

The tomb is situated in the Valley of the Kings at Thebes.

Plan of Tutankhamun's tomb. Because he died young and unexpectedly, his own tomb in the Valley of the Kings was not ready for him, so he was buried in a tomb meant for a noble.

The solid gold funeral mask of Tutankhamun, inlaid with semi-precious stones and coloured glass.

The second of Tutankhamun's two wooden coffins, all covered with gold and semi-precious stones.

Tutankhamun's tomb

'At first I could see nothing, the hot air escaping from the chamber, causing the candle flame to flicker but presently, as my eyes grew accustomed to the light, details of the room within emerged slowly from the mist; strange animals, statues and gold – everywhere the glint of gold ... and when Lord Carnarvon, unable to stand the suspense any longer, inquired anxiously, "Can you see anything?" it was all I could do to get out the words, 'Yes, wonderful things!"'

These famous words belong to Howard Carter who, with his wealthy patron, Lord Carnarvon, discovered the tomb of Tutankhamun. The year was 1922 and Carter had spent 10 years searching for the tomb in the Valley of the Kings. This was expected to be the last season's digging because Lord Carnarvon was to stop paying for the work after that year. Other historians said there was nothing left to be found in the valley. But Carter decided to explore an area covered with rubble from the tomb of Ramesses VI. Beneath the rubble were 16 steps which led to a sealed door and on it was the name of Tutankhamun. Carter and Carnarvon had found a door which had been closed for 3,300 years. What were they to find beyond it?

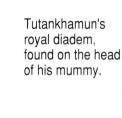

Tutankhamun's royal diadem, found on the head of his mummy.

Tutankhamun's gold pectoral, or pendant, decorated with semi-precious stones and glass paste. In the centre is the winged scarab beetle which was the symbol of the sun god. It is 14.9 centimetres high.

One of the four small coffins which contained the mummified internal organs of Tutankhamun. Each was a miniature version of the second coffin which held the pharaoh's body. It is only 39 centimetres high.

Two life-size statues of Tutankhamun found guarding the entrance to his burial chamber. They are made from wood covered with black varnish, plaster and covered with gold-leaf.

Tutankhamun as a boy, carved from wood and painted.

Fact File

Wonderful things!

'Not a single square inch of floor remains vacant,' wrote Carter. The 'wonderful things' he had seen through a hole in the door were everywhere and it was years before all the objects were taken to their new home in the Cairo Museum. Tutankhamun's three coffins were opened in 1926, each one more spectacular than the first. The final coffin was of solid gold and weighed 110kg (296 lb) – the largest piece of ancient gold ever found! Historians are puzzled. Why, if he was an unimportant pharaoh who died too young to have achieved much, was Tutankhamun buried with such wealth when other, greater pharaohs, were given simple burials?

Inside the tomb was plenty of food for Tutankhamun in the afterlife! Here are mummified joints of meat piled in boxes under a couch.

WRITING AND ART

Writing

The Ancient Egyptians developed a style of writing at the very beginning of their civilization, 5,000 years ago. The Greeks called Egyptian writing hieroglyphics which meant 'sacred carvings', and this is the word used today. Hieroglyphics were used by the Egyptians for 3,400 years until about 1,600 years ago (about AD 400) when they died out. At this point the recorded history of Egypt died too and it would have remained forgotten had we not found out how to read the ancient writing again.

In 1799, French soldiers discovered a broken stone at Rosetta, in the north of Egypt. On the stone was the same passage of text written in two languages: Greek and Egyptian. Scholars studied the stone, convinced it would lead to the unravelling of Ancient Egypt's language. Then, in 1822, Jean-François Champollion, a French scholar of ancient languages, announced that he had succeeded in reading the hieroglyphics by making a careful comparison of the words on the Rosetta Stone.

Egyptian hieroglyphics were pictures used to represent sounds, not actual words. Depending on how a word was pronounced would decide which hieroglyphic pictures to use. Champollion understood this important point and our reading of hieroglyphics today is based on his work. Even though we can now read hieroglyphics, we still do not know how the Ancient Egyptian language was pronounced – this is just one of the many unsolved mysteries about Ancient Egypt.

The Rosetta Stone was carved in 196 BC. Champollion worked out the name 'Ptolemy' and this led him to decipher the writing of the Ancient Egyptians. The text records the gift of land to the temples by the pharaoh Ptolemy V.

Khufu   Akhenaten   Tutankhamun   Hatshepsut   Cleopatra

Royal cartouches. Before Champollion discovered how to read hieroglyphics in 1822, another Frenchman, in 1761, had recognized that hieroglyphics inside these oval shapes were the names of pharaohs.

The Egyptian alphabet contained 24 basic signs, which could be written from right to left, left to right or from top to bottom. Here are 18 of the basic hieroglyphic signs and their meanings.

Read it yourself

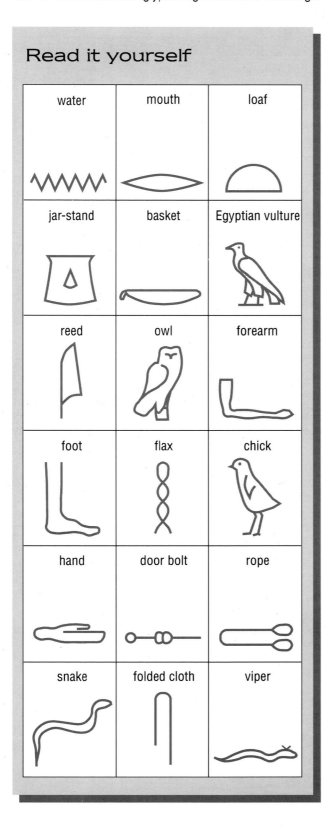

water	mouth	loaf
jar-stand	basket	Egyptian vulture
reed	owl	forearm
foot	flax	chick
hand	door bolt	rope
snake	folded cloth	viper

Fact File

Papyrus

For a language which has been dead for 1,600 years there's a lot of it still around. Statues, temples and tombs are full of carved inscriptions and the dryness of the climate has preserved pieces of papyrus. This is a sort of paper made from reeds of the River Nile. The stems were split and flattened out, side by side. More were laid on top, in the other direction. They too were flattened and the 'mat' of squashed reeds stuck together to make a sheet. When it was dry it was used as writing paper. Many papyrus documents have survived, from shopping lists and letters to royal decrees and spells, such as those from the 'Book of the Dead' (see page 24).

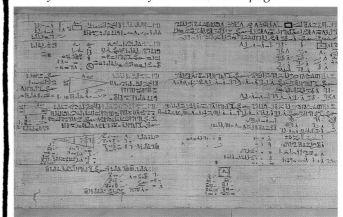

Written document on papyrus. It contains mathematical problems and answers.

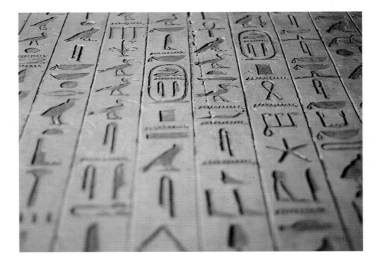

Hieroglyphics carved on the wall of the burial chamber of a pharaoh's pyramid. Look for the pharaoh's name carved inside two cartouches.

Painting and sculpture

Artists were important and skilled people. Painters, sculptors, jewellers, goldsmiths and potters were all part of the artistic community.

When we look at Ancient Egyptian civilization today, it is the work of the painters and sculptors which we find easiest to recognize because of the distinctive 'stiff styles' they created.

Egyptian paintings might look strange to us, but they made perfect sense to the Egyptians. This is because the painters did not paint as they actually saw things, but as they imagined them to be. The result is a highly 'stylized' picture which can be 'read' like the pages in a book. Each animal and human figure in a painting is usually there for a reason, not just for decoration. To understand Egyptian paintings experts have to look for clues to help them – just as a detective must look for clues to help solve his puzzles.

An Egyptian painter did not know about perspective (the art of distorting the shape of something to make it look as if it is seen from the distance). Without perspective all the parts of the human body were drawn as if the painter were looking straight at them. If you tried to stand like a figure in an Egyptian painting, you would fall over!

Stone quarried from rocky outcrops along the Nile was carved into statues by sculptors. They used simple tools of copper and stone.

Colossal statue of Ramesses II.

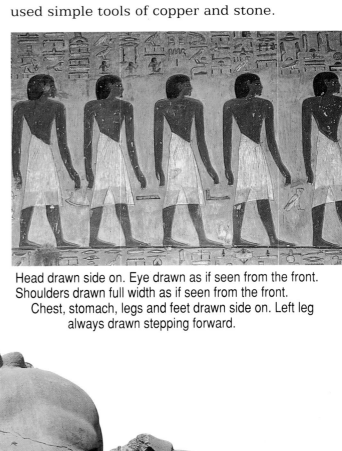

Head drawn side on. Eye drawn as if seen from the front. Shoulders drawn full width as if seen from the front. Chest, stomach, legs and feet drawn side on. Left leg always drawn stepping forward.

Fact File

A painter's work

There are paintings everywhere. On the walls of tombs, inside temples, on coffins and even on pieces of furniture. There must have been thousands and thousands of painters in Ancient Egypt! This is how they worked. First, a small painting was made on a squared background. This was copied square by square on to bigger squares on, say, the wall of a tomb. Then it was coloured in with paints made from pigments. Red, yellow and brown were made from ochre (a type of earth), black came from soot, white from limestone, green from copper ore and blue from powdered quartz.

Egyptian painting from a tomb at Thebes. From left to right the women are holding a palm frond with dates, a vine with black grapes and a lotus flower.

Egyptian painting from a tomb at Thebes. Beneath the two carpenters who are making a bed is a man sitting beside a small furnace. He is making a metal dish. Beneath him are two men polishing a large storage jar.

THE END OF ANCIENT EGYPT

Egypt under the Greeks and Romans

Ancient Egypt didn't just vanish over night – it disappeared gradually until many of its greatest achievements were absorbed by the Greeks and Romans into their worlds.

The Greeks came to Egypt at the end of the 7th century BC. This was a time of Greek expansion. Colonies were being established away from Greece, and Egypt was absorbed into the Greek empire. A Greek city was built in the north of Egypt and named after Alexander the Great, the soldier who claimed the country for Greece. The city was called Alexandria. For the next 250 years the rulers of Egypt were of Greek origin. Greek was their language and it was used for official business. As time passed, fewer people could read the traditional writing of Egypt, hieroglyphics. It was during the time of Greek rule that the Rosetta Stone was carved, with an inscription in both Greek and Egyptian (see page 38).

The Romans came to Egypt in the 1st century BC and their domination lasted for nearly 400 years. Both the Romans and the Greeks introduced their own gods and gave new names to many of the old Egyptian gods.

Egyptian culture adopted Greek and Roman ways. But in return the Greeks and Romans inherited many aspects of Egyptian civilization. Egyptian buildings and art influenced them and some customs were taken up. In the 600 years of Greek and then Roman occupation, the older Egyptian way of life disappeared.

Mummy of a young man from the Roman period. The painting on his coffin board shows him wearing Roman clothes.

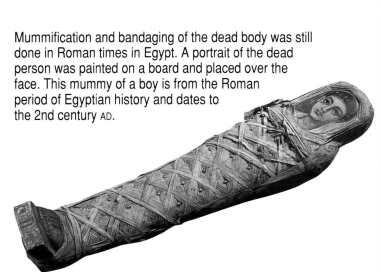

Mummification and bandaging of the dead body was still done in Roman times in Egypt. A portrait of the dead person was painted on a board and placed over the face. This mummy of a boy is from the Roman period of Egyptian history and dates to the 2nd century AD.

View of the interior of the Graeco-Roman catacombs (underground burial chambers) of Kom esh Shougafa, Alexandria, where the traditional Ancient Egyptian funerary carvings continued to be used long after the rule of the pharaohs' ended.

Fact File

Christianity

It all happened so fast! For nearly 3,000 years the pharaohs had been worshipped as gods on Earth. And then in the 1st century AD all this changed as word of a new religion called Christianity spread quickly along the length of the River Nile. The Roman governors of Egypt tried to stamp Christianity out, but they couldn't. A sign was adopted by the early Egyptian Christians to show that they were followers of the teachings of Jesus Christ. The old hieroglyphic sign for 'life', called the 'ankh', was chosen because it looked like a Christian cross with a loop at the top.

The ankh sign.

The modern city of Alexandria with the remains of a Roman theatre.

Discovering Ancient Egypt

The pharaohs of Ancient Egypt wanted to live for ever. This was why they believed in an afterlife, had their dead bodies mummified and were buried with all their worldly goods in strong buildings, such as pyramids and tombs cut into solid rock. Their world died out with the coming of the Greeks and the Romans, but today people want to find out what Ancient Egypt was really like.

Over the past 200 years people have gone to Egypt to discover the ancient civilization for themselves. The pyramids have been entered, tombs have been found in the Valley of the Kings, hieroglyphics have been deciphered, museums have been created and great collections of Egyptian objects have been formed in cities all over the world.

The work of historians continues today. Because the Ancient Egyptian civilization lasted for so long and its remains have survived so well, there are discoveries still to be made. Perhaps there is another burial chamber inside the pyramid of Khufu; there probably are more tombs hidden in the Valley of the Kings; and what information is still to be learned from the many unread papyrus documents which are in museums or buried in the sand of the Egyptian desert ... waiting to be found?

Egyptologists at Manchester Museum unwrapping a mummy.

Egyptian workers helping on an excavation in the desert.

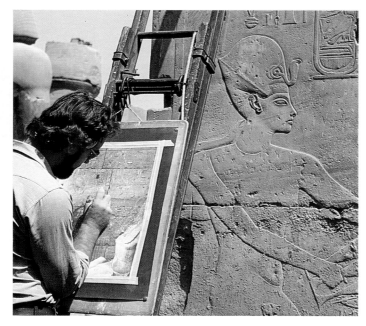

An Egyptologist at work today, making a copy of an inscription.

Fact File

Obelisks

An obelisk was a tapering needle-like stone monument. Its tip was in the shape of a pyramid, covered in a thin layer of gold. The golden tip shone in the sunlight. An obelisk was a symbol of the sun god. Pairs of obelisks were set up in front of temples. Most have been taken down and moved elsewhere. The Romans took so many there are more obelisks in Rome than in Egypt! London, Paris and New York have Egyptian obelisks too. The one in London is called Cleopatra's Needle.

Cleopatra's Needle, London.

GLOSSARY

Abydos – The most important of all Egyptian cemeteries.

Afterlife – The place where the spirit of a dead person would live for ever.

Akhenaten – A pharaoh of the 18th Dynasty who made many daring changes in Egyptian society. Reigned 1353–1335 BC.

Alexander the Great (356–323 BC) – The Greek soldier who claimed Egypt for the Greek empire.

Alexandria – The city built by the Greeks in the north of Egypt.

Anubis – The god who led the spirit of a dead person to the afterlife.

Aten – The sun god whom Akhenaten worshipped.

Bastet – The goddess of cats.

Book of the Dead – A book of spells for use in the afterlife.

Canopic jars – Special jars which held the mummified organs of a dead person.

Lord Carnarvon (1866–1923) – The wealthy patron of Egyptologist Howard Carter.

Howard Carter (1874–1939) – The English Egyptologist who discovered the tomb of Tutankhamun in 1922.

Cartouche – An oval shape inside which was written the name of a pharaoh.

Jean-François Champollion (1790–1832) – The Frenchman who deciphered hieroglyphics.

Cleopatra's Needle – The obelisk in London.

Deir el-Medina – A workers' village near the Valley of the Kings.

Dynasty – The family group into which pharaohs can be placed. There were 31 dynasties in total.

Faience – A blue or green-glazed material made from clay and quartz sand.

Fertile strip – The narrow piece of farming land which runs the length of the River Nile.

Giza – The place near modern Cairo where the best preserved group of pyramids is to be seen. The Sphinx is here, too.

Hatshepsut – A queen in the 18th Dynasty. Reigned 1473–1458 BC.

Hieroglyphics – Ancient Egyptian writing.

Horus – The god who acted as a guide in the afterlife. He was closely linked with the pharaoh.

Imhotep – The prime minister and architect to the pharaoh Djoser. He built the first pyramid, called the Step Pyramid.

Isis – The goddess who protected children. She was the wife of Osiris and mother of Horus.

Karnak – The place where the great temple of Amun-Re is to be seen.

Kemet – The name the Ancient Egyptians called their land. It meant 'the Black Land' which referred to the colour of the soil along the fertile strip.

Lapis lazuli – A blue-coloured semi-precious stone imported into Egypt, valued in jewellery-making.

Lower Egypt – The area in the north of the country.

Mastaba – A type of platform-shaped tomb in use before pyramids. From the Arabic word for 'bench'.

Menes – Egypt's first pharaoh (as far as we know).

Mummy – The preserved body of a dead person, specially treated and wrapped in bandages.

Nagada – A large cemetery in use before the time of the pharaohs.

Narmer – Possibly another name for pharaoh Menes.

Natron – A natural salt used to embalm bodies.

Nefertiti – Wife of Akhenaten.

Obelisk – A tall, pointed stone sometimes decorated with hieroglyphics. A symbol of the sun god.

Osiris – The god who acted as a judge in the afterlife.

Palette – A flat stone for mixing paint or make-up.

Papyrus – Writing paper made from reeds.

Pharaoh – A ruler or king of Ancient Egypt.

Punt – Thought to be modern-day Somalia.

Pyramid – A four-sided tomb for a pharaoh. Most, but not all, had even, triangular sides.

Re – The god who symbolized the sun.

Rosetta Stone – The stone inscribed in Greek and Egyptian which Champollion used to decipher hieroglyphics in the early 19th century.

Sphinx – A strange lion-man figure.

Tell el-Amarna – The modern name for the city Akhetaten built by Akhenaten in the desert.

Thoth – The god of learning and science who is said to have invented writing.

Tutankhamun – A minor pharaoh of the 18th Dynasty. Reigned 1333–1323 BC.

Upper Egypt – The area in the south of the country.

Ushabti – A little figure, usually made of stone, wood or faience buried with a dead person and whose job it was to work for that person in the afterlife.

Valley of the Kings – A valley in which many pharaohs had their tombs, cut into the rock during the New Kingdom.

Vizier – The most important official in the government.